OUR LADY

and

MARIE BERNADETTE SOUBIROUS
(1844-1879)

By Rev. Lawrence G. Lovasik, S.V.D.
Divine Word Missionary

NIHIL OBSTAT: Daniel V. Flynn, J.C.D., *Censor Librorum*

IMPRIMATUR: ✝ Joseph T. O'Keefe, D.D., *Vicar General, Archdiocese of New York*

CPSIA   January 2014   10 9 8 7 6 5 4   A/P

Bernadette's parents were poor.

Bernadette's Home

BERNADETTE Soubirous was born on January 7, 1844, near Lourdes, in France. Her parents were very poor. Her father was a miller. He lost the mill and had to do odd jobs around town while his wife worked in the fields.

By this time Bernadette was five years old, and already looked after the house and cared for her younger brothers and sisters.

The family was forced to move to a rent-free single room of a very old building which once had been a town jail. It was here that Bernadette got asthma in the damp cell in Lourdes, so she was often sent to stay with friends, the Aravants, in the town of Bartres. There she helped with the housework and tended the sheep in the pasture. In return she received her board and lodging. In the evenings Madame Aravant taught her the catechism, the only education she ever received.

At the age of thirteen Bernadette was home again and being prepared for her First Holy Communion.

Bernadette Sees a Lady in the Grotto

BERNADETTE was a good-natured little girl, small for her age. She had big dark eyes and rather stubborn round face. She was very devout.

On Thursday, February 11, 1858, when Bernadette was fourteen, she dressed warmly, for it was a bitterly cold day, and went collecting wood with her small sister and playmate. The two smaller girls ran on ahead, leaving Bernadette behind trying to make up her mind whether or not to wade across the Gave River.

While she was taking off her shoes and stockings, she heard a sound of wind like a storm. She looked all around, but everything was still. There was no movement in the trees. She heard the wind again and looked toward the cave. Then she noticed that a wild rose which was growing below the cave was shaking. The cave was filled with golden light.

Bernadette went to collect wood with two companions.

5

Lifting up her eyes, she saw in the opening of the grotto nearby a lady of great beauty, dressed in a pure white robe with a blue sash, a veil over her head, a rosary clasped in her hands, and yellow roses at her feet. The lady smiled at Bernadette, and asked her to say her rosary.

Mary's purpose in appearing to Bernadette was to warn the child to pray and make sacrifices for sinners. The many miracles of body and soul performed at Lourdes are the proof that this message was a true warning from the Queen of heaven to her children and that she is deeply interested in their welfare.

As a nun, Bernadette wrote a letter describing her experience. "I had gone down one day with two other girls to the bank of the river Gave when suddenly I heard a kind of rustling sound. I turned my head toward the field by the side of the river but the tree seemed quite still and the noise was not from there. Then I looked up and saw a cave where I saw a lady wearing a lovely white dress with a bright blue belt. On top of each of her feet was a pale yellow rose, the same color as her rosary beads.

Bernadette saw a very beautiful lady.

This is the way Bernadette described her vision:

"I RUBBED my eyes, thinking I was seeing things, and I put my hand into the fold of my dress where my rosary was. I wanted to make the sign of the cross but I could not, and my hand just fell down.

"The lady made the sign of the cross herself and then I was able to do the same, though my hands were trembling. Then I began to say the rosary while the lady let her beads slip through her fingers, without moving her lips. When I stopped saying the Hail Mary, she vanished.

"I asked my two companions if they had noticed anything, but they said no. I told them that I had seen a lady wearing a nice white dress, though I didn't know who she was. I told them not to say anything about it. They said I was silly to have anything to do with it. I told them they were wrong. I came back next Sunday, feeling myself drawn to the place."

Bernadette was fourteen when she saw the lady.

"THE third time I went the lady spoke to me and asked me to come every day for fifteen days. I said I would. Then she said that she wanted me to tell the priests to build a chapel there. She also told me to drink from the stream. I went to the Gave, the only stream I could see. She pointed to a little trickle of water nearby. When I got to it I could find only a few drops of water. I began to scrape and was able to get a little water. Three times I threw it away, and the fourth time I was able to drink some. Then the lady vanished and I went back home.

"I went back each day for fifteen days and each time, except one Monday and one Friday, the lady appeared and told me to look for a stream and wash in it and to see that the priests build a chapel there."

The lady told Bernadette to wash in the stream. 11

12   The lady said, ''I am the Immaculate Conception.''

"I must also pray, she said, for the conversion of sinners. I asked her many times what she meant by that, but she only smiled."

On March 25, the Lady answered Bernadette's question as to who she was with the words, "I am the Immaculate Conception." This was said in the Lourdes dialect in which both Bernadette and her Vision spoke.

Bernadette continues:

"Finally, with outstretched arms and eyes looking up to heaven she told me she was the Immaculate Conception.

"During the fifteen days she told me three secrets but I was not to speak about them to anyone, and so far I have not."

Bernadette went back to the grotto every day for two weeks having been told to do so by her Vision, and she talked with the Lady whom she saw there. Thereafter she saw her Vision only a few more times, and after July never again.

Bernadette speaks with her pastor.

Bernadette Tells the Lady's Name

BERNADETTE at once hurried to the pastor's rectory and burst in on the surprised priest Abbé Peyramale. She said, "I am the Immaculate Conception!"

"What? What's that?"

"Monsieur le Curé, the Lady at Massabielle said, 'I am the Immaculate Conception.' "

"What are you talking about? No one can have a name like that. You are making it up. Do you know the meaning of those words?"

Bernadette shook her head.

"Then why say something you don't understand?"

"But I'm only telling you what the Lady told me . . . and I've said the words over and over again so that I would be sure to get them right."

As soon as the priest heard these words, he said to Bernadette, "My child, go home now. I will speak to you another time."

As soon as the door closed behind the girl, the Abbé fell to his knees, and with hands that shook, covered his face.

Crowds of People Go to the Grotto

BERNADETTE'S daily visits to the grotto during that February caused a great stir in the district. Day after day crowds of people from the surrounding countryside followed her to the grotto to watch as she was drawn into long ecstasies. They watched her strange movements as she obediently did the things the lady told her to do, known to her alone. They watched as she scraped away some soil from beside the grotto until a spring of water was trickling out, a spring which provided 27,000 gallons of pure fresh water a day, as it still does. This is the Lourdes water which, just occasionally, brings about miraculous cures.

Bernadette was questioned over and over by her crowd of curious followers as to just what she saw, what the Lady was like, what she said. Soon the police started questioning her, and all the civil authorities.

Little Bernadette kept to her first description, no matter how they tried to catch her in a lie to prove that the vision was only in her imagination.

Crowds of people followed Bernadette to the grotto. **17**

Bernadette at School

BERNADETTE was so pestered with questions that her family thought it better for her to leave home and go to the Sisters of Nevers, who had a school and a hospital in Lourdes. During her five years there she learned to read and write, and she grew a little, and she could answer the questions of the people whose questions had to be answered.

Bernadette was called to answer questions before the episcopal commission on December 7, 1860. Bishop Laurence who was in charge said, "Bernadette, tell us just once more what happened when you asked the Lady her name."

The face of the now sixteen-and-a-half year old girl changed. Extending her arms, she crossed them over her chest, lifted her eyes toward the ceiling and breathed: "She said, 'I am the Immaculate Conception.' "

As Bishop Laurence lookd at Bernadette's radiant face, tears rolled down his cheeks. He afterwards said to the other priests, "Did you see that child? Did you see her face?"

The Sisters of Nevers teach Bernadette.

Bernadette becomes a novice.

Bernadette Enters the Convent

SIX years later, so as to get away from the public eye, Bernadette became a nun of the Order of the Sisters of Charity of Nevers and moved to their convent in that city. She left Lourdes and the Pyrenees forever. Now she began to live a hidden life.

Three years later the Bishop put the novice's veil on Bernadette and gave her the name she would be known by in religion, Sister Marie-Bernard.

After this ceremony Bernadette was assigned to help out in the infirmary and in the sacristy. At the same time she followed the exercises of the novitiate with fervor. She had some free time; this she spent in prayer and reading.

She was humble enough to talk about her faults. She said, "I have a sharp tongue and a quick temper, and, of course, I want to give orders. Perhaps because I had charge of my little brothers at home. I have been stubborn all my life. Even at the Grotto I had to be told three times by Our Lady to drink the water."

22   **Bernadette in the convent infirmary.**

Bernadette Becomes Ill

THE Reverend Mother and the Mistress of Novices were often harsh with her because they tried to humble her. Some asked her whether she did not feel proud, but she answered, "But I was just used. The Virgin used me as a broom to remove dust. When the work is done the broom is put behind the door again."

Bernadette had always been delicate and had had the Anointing of the Sick three times. But in the last year of her life, when only thirty five years old, she developed a swelling and endured great suffering. Unable to sleep at night, gasping for breath, sick and full of pain, she prayed, "O Jesus, when I see Your cross, I forget my own." And by day, longing to be up and at work, she learned to say, "I am at my work." If she was asked, "What is it?" she would answer, "Being sick."

Bernadette said, "When one is a bride of Jesus Christ, in any physical or mental pain one must say only 'yes, my God,' without any 'ifs' or 'buts.'"

The Death of Bernadette

ON December 8, the feast of the Immaculate Conception, Bernadette went to the chapel for the last time; three days later she became bed-ridden. Asthma, tuberculosis, severe bleeding, and the tumor on the knee, all caused her great pain.

Bernadette said to the sister who was nursing her, "Do not pay any attention to my suffering. I suffer, but I am glad to suffer. I'm prepared to put up with anything for Jesus, anything to help save sinners."

On March 20 she was anointed. Afterwards she said to the Mother General: "Please Mother, please forgive me. Ever since I have been here I have caused trouble. Will you tell my companions that I am asking their forgiveness for the bad example that I have set them?"

Three sisters knelt at her side and prayed the "Hail Mary." At the words, "Holy Mary," Bernadette joined in. "Mother of God . . . pray for me . . . poor sinner . . . poor, poor sinner."

Then she breathed her last breath.

Bernadette dies saying, "Holy Mary, Mother of God." 25

The Incorrupt Body of Bernadette

BERNADETTE died, worn out with suffering, on April 16, 1879 at the age of thirty-six.

So deep was the memory of the beauty of Our Lady, that Bernadette, many years later in her sick bed at the convent, could still say, "When you have seen her once, you just long to die so that you can see her again."

Bernadette's longing had now come true. She could see again the beauty of the Immaculate Virgin Mary whom she loved so much on earth.

So many people filed past her body, as it lay in state in the convent chapel at Nevers, that funeral arrangements had to be delayed. Mother General insisted that Sister Marie-Bernard should be buried, not in the town cemetery, but in the chapel of St. Joseph which stood in the garden. It was beneath this chapel that a tomb was built for her.

Bernadette's incorrupt body in the convent chapel.   27

Bernadette Is Declared a Saint

O N August 20, 1908, an ecclesiastical court was set up to study the case for her beatification. One of the first tasks of the court was to exhume Bernadette's body. After being buried for over thirty years, it was found to be incorrupt.

Her head inclined slightly to the left. Her arms crossed over her chest, still clasped her crucifix and rosary. Both were tarnished and full of rust.

The flesh was white and intact, and her parted lips were smiling.

On May 13, 1913, Pope Pius X signed the decree introducing the cause of Bernadette's beatification. She was beatified on June 14th, 1925. Eight years later, on the feast of the Immaculate Conception, December 8, 1933 she was canonized by Pope Pius XI.

During the process of the canonization Pope Pius XI wrote: "We are pleased to say, for the greater glory of God, this life can be summed

up in three words. Bernadette was *faithful* to her mission, she was *humble* in glory, and she was *valiant* in her sufferings."

Now her incorrupt body can be seen as she lies in death in the side chapel of the mother-house of the Sisters of Charity at Nevers, where she lived and died as Sister Marie-Bernard.

Lourdes Today

LOURDES today remains one of the most frequented of Christian shrines. More than three million visitors, pilgrims and tourists, come each year to the Grotto of Massabielle, where the Virgin Mary appeared to Bernadette eighteen times in 1858. Many visitors devote a whole day or several days to their pilgrimage. They meet thousands of men, women, children, sick people, young and old from all nations and races, who help them in their search for God, and to bring their lives more in keeping with the message of poverty, prayer, penance, purity and dedication preached by Bernadette in her life.

Lourdes has three basilicas: the Basilica of the Immaculate Conception built over the grotto with its crypt, the Basilica of the Holy Rosary with its fifteen chapels and mosaics of the fifteen mysteries of the Rosary, and the Basilica of Pope St. Pius X built underground for large gatherings. Ten acres of buildings and religious monuments, hospital, museum and conference rooms are maintained by 150 people.

**The Basilica of the Immaculate Conception
and the Holy Rosary.**

Prayer of the Church

GOD, protector and lover of the humble,
You bestowed upon Your servant,
   Bernadette,
the favor of beholding the Immaculate Virgin
   Mary
and of talking with her.
Grant that we may deserve
to behold You in heaven.